For Love of The Book

An Introduction to God's Word

Copyright © 2018 Rodger Copp

All rights reserved. This book or any portion thereof may not be reproduced or used in any manner whatsoever without express written permission.

ISBN 978-0-9988041-0-1

Scripture quotations: The Holy Bible
                               King James Version
                               1611 Edition

Cover photograph: Korsmo Creations Photography
                                   Northwood, ND

Printed and bound in the USA
SmartPress
950 Lake Drive
Chanhassen, MN 55317
https://smartpress.com

Published by Rodger Copp
Bayfield, WI 54814
ftlotbook@gmail.com

For additional copies visit:

http://forloveofthebook.com

For Love of The Book

An Introduction to God's Word

Rodger Copp

"A Bible that's falling apart usually belongs to someone who isn't."

— Charles H. Spurgeon

Contents

Introduction

I. Why is the Bible Important? 3
    God's Word Preserves People and Nations 3
    God's Word Reveals That Which Is Hidden 5

II. Introduction to God's Word 9
    Characteristics of the Bible 9
    Satisfying the Need to Know God 14

III. The Bible's Origins 15
    Scribal Duties 18
    The Essenes 19
    The Samaritans 20

IV. Bible Translation Timeline 21

V. What Others Have Said 31

VI. How Can the Bible Be Understood? 35
    Know the Gospel 36
        Jesus Paid the Penalty 36
        The Exodus Passover Archetype 36
        The New Testament Fulfillment 37
        The Resurrection is Proof! 37
        Are You Sure? 37
    Develop a Habit 41
    Scripture Explains Itself 41
    Commentaries 42
    Go to Church 42
    Bible Software 42
    An Audio Bible 42

Conclusion 44

Early North American Bibles 47

References 50

"If there is anything in my thoughts or style to commend, the credit is due to my parents for instilling in me an early love of the Scriptures. If we abide by the principles taught in the Bible, our country will go on prospering and to prosper; but if we and our posterity neglect its instructions and authority, no man can tell how sudden a catastrophe may overwhelm us and bury all our glory in profound obscurity."

— Daniel Webster

Introduction

The world is in the midst of moral crisis, and the situation is worsening. The Word of God is the only hope for preserving the lives and eternal destinies of all — men and women, boys and girls. Those who do not have a relationship with the Lord must be introduced to Him. We who know Him must realize that the Bible is God speaking to us; we need to listen, believe, and obey.

Ezekiel 18 makes it clear that *God does not want us to suffer the consequences of sin.* The Bible is a light shining into the smallest corners of our being, enabling us to recognize our sin. Once we are aware of our iniquity, we have an opportunity to seek forgiveness and avoid recurrence. If we are diligent in keeping our lives pure, we will reap splendid benefits. If we choose to ignore God and the Bible, we will experience all sorts of difficulties in life and unspeakable suffering after death.

This book presents a brief history of the Bible. Included are some of the Bible's unique characteristics and details about its rendering into English. Those involved in the translations volunteered for the front lines of a spiritual war. We are indebted to them because of their willingness to risk all they had — yes, even their lives — so that we could have the Bible we have today. The evidence is undeniable; they believed and practiced Matthew 6:19 - 20:

> *"Lay not up for yourselves treasures upon earth . . . But lay up for yourselves treasures in heaven,"*
> *— Jesus Christ*

My intention is that this book be a tool for telling people about God's Good News. Are you willing to help spread the Word? You can start by giving this book to someone when you are finished.

I encourage you to purchase additional copies of this book to give to others. To purchase copies, go to the web address found on the copyright page. Start laying up your treasures in Heaven!

Lord,

May it become apparent to the reader that all Scripture originated with You and passed to the minds, pens, and parchments of faithful men. Help us to realize the pressing need to believe Your Book.

Because of Jesus, let it be so.

I

WHY IS THE BIBLE IMPORTANT?

God's Word Preserves People and Nations

Preservation is the investment of resources to keep something from destruction. Some years ago, I was using word scrambles regularly in my Sunday school class. One morning the word "preservation" crossed my mind, and I needed to know what words were hiding inside it. An online unscramble tool rewarded me with the answer. On the first line of a long list of possibilities were the words "savior" and "repent." I was awestruck by that perfect *coincidence*.

God made the ultimate investment to make our preservation possible. He sent Jesus Christ, His only Son, to be the Savior of mankind. His Word offers us the opportunity to trust Him. Two of the most significant purposes of the Bible are to make us aware of our need and to explain how our sins can be forgiven. The preservation of our physical life and of our eternal souls depends on our changing our mind about Jesus Christ and our sin, also called repentance, and believing what Christ did for us.

Pew Research Center conducted a survey in 2014 to determine the beliefs held by various religious groups.

Of those professing Christian faiths, 37% take the Bible literally, and approximately the same percentage believes that clear standards of right and wrong exist.

Considering humanity's collective ethics, who doubts morality must improve? Unfortunately, if 63% of Christians believe that no absolute standards exist for behavior, society will continue to degenerate. Second President of the United States John Adams said, "Our Constitution was made only for a moral and religious people. It is wholly inadequate to the government of any other."

Will people become moral and religious if left to themselves? No, they will not. Without outside influence, nature insists on increasing disorder, or in this case, escalating immorality. Man's depravity is getting worse by the day. The further we get from God, the closer we get to societal collapse.

A nation of free people cannot exist indefinitely unless its citizens live to a high moral standard. Force cannot maintain a constitutional republic. If coercion becomes necessary, the result will be something other than a government of, by, and for the people. America will be preserved only if a righteous people fulfill their God-given directive of being salt (preservative) and light (Matthew 5:13-16).

There is another reason why the Bible is important.

God's Word Reveals That Which Is Hidden

The Bible refers to Jesus Christ, to Itself, and to Christians as *instruments of light*. Some of these references are metaphors illustrating the similarity between a light that reveals what is hidden in the dark, and a spiritual luminary that exposes the darkness of sin. By our nature, we want to keep our sin secret, and we are extremely sensitive to anything that might reveal our misdeeds.

"And this is the condemnation, that light is come into the world, and men loved darkness rather than light, because their deeds were evil.

For every one that doeth evil hateth the light, neither cometh to the light, lest his deeds should be reproved."

—John 3: 19, 20

"But all things that are reproved are made manifest by the light: for whatsoever doth make manifest is light."

—Ephesians 5:13

Our laws sometimes uncover wrongdoing, but they have limitations. Without witnesses or sufficient evidence, malefactions will occur with impunity. Human regulations cannot possibly condemn the superabundance of secret sins that are visible only to the all-seeing Eye of our Creator. His Word is designed to expose the dark crevices of iniquity, and His Word will bear sin's penalties to our consciousness.

"For the word of God is quick, and powerful, and sharper than any twoedged sword, piercing even to the dividing asunder of soul and spirit, and of the joints and marrow, and is a discerner of the thoughts and intents of the heart."
—Hebrews 4:12

The Word of God is the Creator's mechanism for revealing sin. When people read the Bible with a willing mind, they will recognize their shortcomings. As they live what they have learned, the following benefits will become evident in their lives, others will benefit, and the Lord receives the glory.

- Priorities change and focus moves from self to others;

- Fairness and truth become a priority;

- Relationships in the family and community improve;

- Courage and boldness flourish when it is time to stand for what is right;

- Responsibility becomes the rule rather than the exception;

- Good behavior takes the place of bad;

- Forgiveness replaces bitterness and hatred.

"The entrance of thy words giveth light; it giveth understanding unto the simple."
—Psalm 119:130

Until the mid-twentieth century, citizens of America and Europe reverenced the Bible. The wise and good knew that the Bible was something special, and the

Scriptures had a tremendous influence on their culture. Regrettably, the morals of this world are not improving. Because of the widespread rejection of God's Word, we have experienced an unhindered decline in principled living. Terrible consequences are already resulting from abandoning God's laws, and the future is bleak indeed if we do not return to Him in repentance and faith.

The Bible contains the only hope for humanity. The solution to every conceivable problem found in the soul of man is in the Bible. Fundamentally, the responsibility for controlling our current moral free fall belongs to God's people. If we ever hope to see this decline reversed, Christians must believe that God is the author of the Bible. Christians must take the Bible literally, commit to its study, and live a life consistent with its standards. The Bible's principles need to occupy our thought-life, and we must live them out each day. If we do our part, the Lord will do His, and everyone will benefit.

"And these words, which I command thee this day, shall be in thine heart:

And thou shalt teach them diligently unto thy children, and shalt talk of them when thou sittest in thine house, and when thou walkest by the way, and when thou liest down, and when thou risest up . . .

And thou shalt write them upon the posts of thy house, and on thy gates."
—Deuteronomy 6:6-9

The Bible is the inerrant Word of God. Its sixty-six books are not a collection of religious writings, advancing certain theories, but they constitute one body, breathing with life and power. From the first verse in Genesis to the last verse in Revelation there is a wonderful continuity of thought, without any clash of opinion; all is a harmonious whole. This fact necessitates one great Author, One who guided the thoughts of each writer and who instructed them to write as they did. This guiding and supervising Author is the Spirit of God."

— Arno C. Gaebelein

II

INTRODUCTION TO GOD'S WORD

Characteristics of the Bible

The Bible is the Word of God. Through it, we are made aware of the Lord's character and expectations. God's Holy Spirit inspired men to write what the Creator wanted us to learn. His message benefits everyone, teaching what needs to be believed and defining the difference between right and wrong. Yes, the Scriptures were written by men — men who were guided by His Holy Spirit, writing His words combined with their style and perspective. The Lord intended the Bible to be the perfect standard for faith and the perfect blueprint for putting faith into practice.

The motivation for having a good grasp of The Book is simple: Those who trust and obey the Bible reap rewards, both now and in eternity. The Bible refers to itself as something more valuable than gold or great wealth, and to treat the Bible as such would benefit us beyond measure. Every person should have a Bible and should read it frequently. Because of the Bible's power to change a person, readers should pray to have the resolve to pattern their lives after it.

*"I rejoice at thy word, as one that findeth **great spoil.**"*

—Psalm 119:162

"The law of the LORD is perfect, converting the soul: the testimony of the LORD is sure, making wise the simple.

The statutes of the LORD are right, rejoicing the heart: the commandment of the LORD is pure, enlightening the eyes.

The fear of the LORD is clean, enduring for ever: the judgments of the LORD are true and righteous altogether.

More to be desired are they than gold, yea, than much fine gold: *sweeter also than honey and the honeycomb."*

—Psalm 19:7-10

The Bible has many characteristics, fingerprints as it were, that help us to understand that it came from God. No other book in history has possessed the harmony, morality, and expression found in the Word of God. The Bible contains many fulfilled prophecies and facts about Creation. Thousands of years passed before the scientific community recognized some of these truths, e.g., the hydrologic cycle and the importance of running water for hygiene.

Furthermore, the following list of Biblical concepts is evidence that men did not work alone as they wrote. This list is light years beyond the scope of naked human reason. When we consider each item's meaning and the obvious insight they all have into the human condition, it is impossible to assail the Creator's inspiration of His Word.

Righteousness and Equity in Moral Absolutes	The Ten Commandments and Other Moral Laws
Creator's Concern for the Fate of Man	Ways to Encourage Ethical Behavior
Instances of God's Mercy	Unbiased Analysis of Humanity
Our Sinful Condition and How to be Forgiven	Distinct Personality of the Genuinely Redeemed
Eventual and Unavoidable Penalty of Immoral Conduct	Heavenly Promises and Their Effect on the Spirit
Reassurances During Difficult Times	Getting Ready for Death

The Bible has two main divisions: the Old Testament and the New Testament. Each consists of individual books that 1. explain the unchanging love and justice of God toward humanity, and 2. point to the Redeemer, Jesus Christ. The events depicted in the New Testament share a distinct uniformity with those of the Old Testament. Rituals, observances, and situations described throughout the Bible often refer to similar circumstances elsewhere.

As you read the Old Testament, keep the New Testament in mind. The Old explains what to expect in the New because the New is the fulfillment of the prophecies and archetypes of the Old. As you become more familiar with the Bible, an extraordinary synergy becomes evident. Not only does this synergy exist between the testaments, but it is found in the individual books as well. The Old, that tells of Christ

Who will come, segues seamlessly into the New that tells of Christ Who has come. Both are essential parts of the whole.

For visual proof of the interconnectedness found in the Bible, google "bible cross-reference data" and examine the graphics created from these data sets. These visualizations are beautiful representations of the reciprocity in the Bible. I believe that these images reveal a marvelous tapestry created by the Master Weaver. To imagine that forty writers over a period of seventeen centuries could have created a document with this level of agreement is difficult — that is, until you realize that God is the Author. I especially liked http://www.chrisharrison.net/index.php/Visualizations/BibleViz.

The Bible speaks of God and His plans for Creation, of man's colossal failure in the Garden, and of man's redemption. If you consider the Bible as one book, the individual parts of the Bible from Genesis to Revelation rely on and uphold one another. Why? *Because each compilation is required to complete God's intended purpose.*

Not only does the Bible tell us *how* to live a morally pure life, but it *insists* that we do — and with the greatest degree of authority. The Word of God goes much further by providing an authentic demonstration of such a life in the person of God the Son, Jesus Christ.

Jesus was the perfect example of emotion and its proper response to any situation. Jesus' speech and behavior were a combination of humility, wisdom, compassion, and holiness such that few comprehended their greatness. By living and loving as only God can, Jesus demonstrated the way to the Father that even a simple person could understand. Those who witnessed His majesty and were willing to acknowledge it and surrender to it knew who He was.

"And Simon Peter answered and said, Thou art the Christ, the Son of the living God."
—Matthew 16:16

The plan of salvation is most apparent in the New Testament for a reason. As news of the gospel spread and churches sprang up, the world learned of redemption. Salvation was no longer the mystery it once was. Faithful men and women shared what Jesus Christ had taught them.

"Jesus saith unto him, I am the way, the truth, and the life: no man cometh unto the Father, but by me."
—John 14:6

God's Word is intended to meet the desires of the soul by providing the answer to *How can I have a relationship with God?* Although some people have hidden the need deep inside and may claim it does not exist, I believe we all desire reconciliation with the Creator. A dominant longing of the human spirit is to know who we are, why we are here, and what is on the other side of death. The only trustworthy source for these answers is that which has been transcribed, guarded, and passed onto us by the Hebrews and the faithful men who worked on the translations.

How Does Someone Satisfy the Need to Know God?

<u>Ask a Simple Question</u>
"And brought them out, and said, Sirs, what must I do to be saved?"

—Acts 16:30

<u>Simply Admit Your Guilt</u>
"He (God) looketh upon men, and if any say, I have sinned, and perverted that which was right, and it profited me not;

He will deliver his soul from going into the pit, and his life shall see the light."

—Job 33:27, 28

<u>Simply Believe</u>
"These things have I written unto you that believe on the name of the Son of God; that ye may know that ye have eternal life, and that ye may believe on the name of the Son of God."

—I John 5:13

<u>Simply Ask Him</u>
"For whosoever shall call upon the name of the Lord shall be saved."

—Romans 10:13

III

THE BIBLE'S ORIGINS

The span of time in which the forty authors wrote the Scriptures encompasses more than seventeen hundred years, from ~1650 BC to AD 90. God miraculously created the tablets containing the Ten Commandments, and Moses delivered them to the people. Moses went on to write the first five books called the Pentateuch, and John wrote Revelation, the last book. The Lord uniquely prepared each writer for his contribution, and He guided them as they put "pen to paper." Each book has a similar and consistent record that supports the others, either by quotes or specific acknowledgments of the prophets, apostles, and the Lord Jesus.

As others contributed to the Hebrew Bible, the work gradually increased in scope and size. The scribes accurately reproduced and protected the Scriptures as they expanded and were passed on.

The following verses provide an idea about how the Bible began:

"And Moses wrote all the words of the LORD, and rose up early in the morning, and builded an altar under the hill, and twelve pillars, according to the twelve tribes of Israel."
—Exodus 24:4

"And he gave unto Moses, when he had made an end of communing with him upon mount Sinai, two tables of testimony, tables of stone, written with the finger of God."

—Exodus 31:18

"And Moses wrote their goings out according to their journeys by the commandment of the LORD: and these are their journeys according to their goings out."

—Numbers 33:2

"And it came to pass, when Moses had made an end of writing the words of this law in a book, until they were finished,"

—Deuteronomy 31:24

"And Joshua wrote these words in the book of the law of God, and took a great stone, and set it up there under an oak, that was by the sanctuary of the LORD"

—Joshua 24:26

"Oh that my words were now written! oh that they were printed in a book!" (They were!)

—Job 19:23

"Moreover the LORD said unto me, Take thee a great roll, and write in it with a man's pen concerning Mahershalalhashbaz."

—Isaiah 8:1

16

"Thus speaketh the LORD God of Israel, saying, Write thee all the words that I have spoken unto thee in a book."
—Jeremiah 30:2

"Then took Jeremiah another roll, and gave it to Baruch the scribe, the son of Neriah; who wrote therein from the mouth of Jeremiah all the words of the book which Jehoiakim king of Judah had burned in the fire: and there were added besides unto them many like words."
—Jeremiah 36:32

"In the first year of Belshazzar king of Babylon Daniel had a dream and visions of his head upon his bed: then he wrote the dream, and told the sum of the matters."
—Daniel 7:1

The kingdom of Judah fell to the Babylonians in approximately 590 BC, and many citizens were exiled to Babylon. As a result, they learned their captors' language. Jewish leaders appointed instructors to teach the Law of Moses so that familiarity with the Scriptures was not forgotten. Near the end of their captivity, Ezra was the administrator of this group of men.

When Cyrus the Great allowed the Jews to leave Babylon, Ezra returned to Jerusalem where he finished arranging the individual books of the Old Testament. Because of Ezra's work and his dedication to restoring worship and obedience to the Scriptures, Israel considered him to be a second Moses. Jewish tradition credits Nehemiah, Ezra, and perhaps others with the development of the Great Synagogue or Great Assembly. For the first time, the Israelites acknowledged the scribes as a unique class in the nation.

Scribal Duties

A scribe was not merely a person who copied documents. In ancient Jewish times, a scribe was also a record keeper and a professional theologian. Among his duties were:

- Make the only authorized copies of the Scriptures.

- Count all the words and letters, the middle word and middle letter in the reproduction, and compare these data to the original.

- Read the Law in public on the Sabbath and festival days.

- Deliver lectures at the colleges during the week.

- Organize events for public worship.

- Preserve the rules that defined how to copy, keep, and interpret the holy writings.

- Correct any inadvertent mistakes found in copies.

- Add the books of the prophets and the poets to the canon.

By 300 BC, the scribes became less prominent in Jewish society, and they allegedly ceased to exist after the death of Simon the Just. The Sages, Wise Ones, Elders, and Doctors eventually replaced the scribes. Their responsibilities were similar, and they performed that function from 200 BC to AD 220.

The Doctors were notable leaders in the nation. Jesus as a twelve-year-old made quite an impression on this group while listening to them, querying them, and providing answers. They were awestruck by Jesus' understanding.

"And it came to pass, that after three days they found him in the temple, sitting in the midst of the doctors, both hearing them, and asking them questions.

And all that heard him were astonished at his understanding and answers."

—Luke 2:46, 47

Essenes

The Essenes were probably the most dedicated group when it came to preserving Scripture. Zealousness and strict adherence to the law defined these people. They denied themselves any comforts enjoyed by others of the same period.

The Essenes are commonly believed to be the source of the Dead Sea Scrolls. In 1946, these scrolls were found in several caves near the Dead Sea. The scrolls contained partial or complete reproductions of each book in the Hebrew Bible, excluding the book of Esther. The scrolls were intact and unused from possibly as early as 300 BC — more than two thousand years ago!

The Samaritans

A study of the Samaritan people will reveal historical evidence of the continuity of Scripture. They separated from the Jews after the Babylonian captivity and created a new belief system using the Five Books of Moses for their Scriptures. Intense religious friction existed between the Jews and the Samaritans. To suggest that they would have cooperated to keep the Scriptures synchronized is highly unlikely. Both groups were eager to persuade everyone that their version of the Law was the oldest. Others have said that the differences between the two versions of Scripture are inconsequential.

One of the goals of this book is to explain how the Holy Scriptures found their way into English. Our lives should demonstrate a strengthened faith when we realize how the Lord directed this process.

"So then faith cometh by hearing, and hearing by the word of God."

—Romans 10:17

IV

BIBLE TRANSLATION TIMELINE

6th c. BC It is possible that the first translation from Hebrew into any other language occurred when the Jews were in Babylon. The Aramaic language found its way into nearly half of the book of Daniel. One Talmud, the Babylonian Talmud, is written in Jewish Babylonian Aramaic. When the Hebrews returned to their homeland, Aramaic was the language used for everyday communication.

3rd c. BC The Septuagint or Greek Old Testament is a translation from the Hebrew to Koine Greek. The work was done in Alexandria, Egypt and is the earliest known translation. As the Jewish people moved throughout the world, Greek eventually became their primary language.

2nd - 3rd c. AD Tertullian spoke of a Latin version of the gospels.

AD 381 St. Jerome was commissioned to translate the whole Bible into Latin, and people referred to it as the Vulgate. The Latin Vulgate became a widely used translation.

AD 383   Ulphilas translated the Bible from Greek into the Gothic language. The Uppsala University Library in Sweden currently holds fragments of the original edition, placed there in 1648.

Another part of this Bible, referred to as the Speyer Fragment, was found in Germany in 1970 and contains the last verses of the Gospel of Mark.

5th c. AD   The Septuagint became the basis for several other translations.

AD 638   Christians traveled from Syria to Sian, China and translated the Hebrew Bible into Chinese.

AD 688   The oldest version of the Anglo-Saxon Gospels is called the Durham Gospels. A single folio of this manuscript is now at Magdalene College, Cambridge.

AD 735   Venerable Bede, an English monk, translated the Gospel of John into English.

AD 862   Two Greek brothers, Cyril and Methodius, along with their students, developed an alphabet for Slavic languages and used it to translate the Bible. This lead to Scripture in the Bulgarian, Serbian, and Russian languages.

9th c. AD   Alfred the Great used Exodus chapters 20 - 23 as the basis for legislation. He desired that "all freeborn youth of the kingdom should be able to read the English Scriptures." He also translated portions of the Bible for his family.

1260 Europe experienced a resurgence of religious zeal in the 13th century. This spiritual renewal resulted in a Norman-French translation of the Bible.

1380 John Wycliffe translated Scriptures from the Latin Vulgate into English. He completed the work in approximately 1384, and others revised the translation after his death. Although now in English, the Bible was not easily accessible. All copies were handwritten, and to possess one was dangerous.

Wycliffe's work played an essential role in opening the way for the Reformation.

Beginning with Wycliffe, the government and church hierarchy cruelly opposed translating the Bible into English. They would do anything and go anywhere to frustrate a translator's work. Their reasons for such persecution can be distilled into one simple quote: "Beware the evil spawned by covetousness."

Discussing the motives for their opposition is beyond the scope of this book. Inquiring minds will obtain the most excellent book, *Wide as the Waters: The Story of the English Bible and the Revolution It Inspired* by Benson Bobrick.

1450 The printing press was perfected in Germany, and Johannes Gutenberg printed the Latin Bible. Bibles became much easier to reproduce, less costly, and more available.

1525-34 William Tyndale translated the Bible from Greek and Hebrew into English and printed his work on the Gutenberg press — a monument to the great learning and ability of the "Captain of the Reformers." He translated the entire New Testament, the Five Books of Moses, the books of Joshua, Judges, Ruth, First and Second Samuel, First and Second Kings, First Chronicles, and Jonah.

He believed the Scriptures had one simple, literal meaning, and he was diligent not to change it. Even those who hated his work admitted it was excellent. Its language was without fault and easily understood. He wrote for the common man, not the scholars, as was so often the case. He was, without a doubt, the father of the English Authorized Version.

The unrelenting hunt for Tyndale ended with a friend's betrayal. The authorities imprisoned him in Vilvoorde Castle, Belgium for over a year. He was convicted of heresy and treason in 1536 and suffered a martyr's death at age 44. Those who attended his execution said his final words were, "Lord! Open the King of England's eyes." His prayer received a quick answer.

Three officially sanctioned printings of the Bible followed within the same number of years.

We would do well to remember three of Tyndale's faithful colleagues, two of whom sacrificed themselves to support his work:

John Fry, who was burned at the stake in London in 1552 because of his assistance with the translation; the Monk William Roye, who was put to death for the same offense in Portugal in 1553; and Myles Coverdale, who barely escaped death in 1554 during the reign of Queen Mary.

Tyndale spent a lifetime using his exceptional literary gifts and skill so that the common man would have access to the Bible in his language.

His quote "If God spare my life, ere many years I will cause a boy that driveth the plough to know more of the Scripture than thou dost," states what was most important to him.

1534 Parliament settled Henry VIII's attempts to separate from the Pope of Rome by establishing the Church of England, with the king declared as the Church's head.

The work of translating and printing the Bible in English began in earnest, which was immensely helpful to those involved in the Reformation.

Martin Luther spent twelve years translating the Bible into the German language.

1535 Myles Coverdale produced the first complete modern-English translation of the entire Bible and the first full printed translation into English. This work was not translated directly from Hebrew and Greek, however, but relied upon the Latin Vulgate, other English and German sources, and Tyndale's work. Coverdale declared that he "had not changed so much as one word for the benefit of any sect, but had with clear conscience purely and faithfully translated out of the foregoing interpreters, having only before his eyes the manifest truth of Scriptures."

Lord Cromwell, chief minister to Henry VIII, preferred Coverdale's edition and convinced the king to publish this decree:

"Every person or proprietary of every parish church within the realm should, before the first of August, 1536, provide a book of the whole Bible, both in Latin and English, and lay it in the choir, for every man that would to look and read therein."

1537 While John Rogers was ministering to English merchants in Antwerp, he met William Tyndale. Under Tyndale's influence, Rogers embraced Tyndale's faith and married.

He continued with Tyndale's work and in 1537, under the pen name of Thomas Matthew, released the Matthew Bible. This Bible combined the work of three men: Tyndale, Coverdale, and Rogers himself.

Rogers was burned at the stake in 1555, the first to die during Queen Mary's reign.

1539 A reprint of the Matthew Bible was released by Richard Taverner, with the support of

King Henry and Lord Cromwell.

Henry VIII sought permission from Francis I of France to print an English Bible in France. Coverdale assumed responsibility for this effort, but the Inquisition defeated the enterprise, burning almost all of the 2500 copies. A few were saved, along with the type and presses. Coverdale completed the work in England in 1539. This Bible became known as the "Great Bible."

1540 After Cromwell died, the Church of Rome gained strength in Parliament. As a result, that body passed a law invalidating Tyndale's version. Those opposed to his work said it was "full of errors and to produce many evils, heresies, and mischiefs, destructive to the harmony and peace of the realm."

1547 Henry the VIII's son, Edward the VI, came to power and lifted the restrictions on having and reading the Bible. Edward became interested in religious matters, and Protestantism was well established for the first time. Under the leadership of Thomas Cranmer, clerical celibacy and the Mass were eliminated, and church services were required to be in English. Before his untimely death, Edward attempted to put protections in place to prevent the country from losing its Protestant advantage, but these failed, leading to Queen Mary's reign.

1553 Queen Mary restored the pre-eminence of the Roman Church in England and in

1555, began a religious purge. In the last three years of her short five-year reign, she executed nearly 400 Protestants, 300 of whom were burned at the stake. Her malignant enthusiasm cemented the fate of the Catholic Church in England. In her attempt to drive out Protestantism, she drove it in. Many scholars and clergy sought refuge in Geneva and, with tremendous effort, continued working on translations.

1560 As was the case for the early church in North Africa, the blood of martyrs became "holy seed." The fruit of Mary's slaughter was the Geneva Bible. Righteous goals combined with freedom often results in tremendous work being accomplished. The people who moved to Switzerland turned the city of Geneva into an energetic hub of Biblical scholarship. The Geneva Bible was the most favored version for eighty-five years and was preferred by the Puritans and Pilgrims. This was the Bible upon which America was founded.

1604-11 The 1611 King James Bible had its beginnings in a conference assembled by the king. The Great Bible and the Bishop's Bible needed work, and the goal was to develop a new translation based on the Bishop's Bible. Forty-seven scholars worked on the project, all of whom were members of the Church of England. A fourth of them had Puritan leanings.

No records exist of the meetings of the translators, but the rules for completing their work were published. Organizers divided the forty-seven into six groups, and each group worked on specific books of the Bible. The committee would select a person to read the Bishop's Bible, while the others followed with a version of Scriptures in the Greek, Hebrew, Aramaic, or Latin languages.

If anyone noticed an error, he spoke up; if not, the reader continued.

The drafts produced by the teams were compared and edited.

The introduction and argument for each book were the work of Thomas Bilson, Bishop of Winchester, and Dr. Miles Smith, who was afterward Bishop of Gloucester. In the preface Dr. Smith wrote, "We, building upon their foundation that went before us, and being holpen[helped] by their labors, do endeavor to make better that which they left so good, no man, we are sure, hath cause to mistake us. They, we persuade ourselves, if they were alive, would thank us." He also said it was their aim ". . . not to make a new translation, nor yet to make of a bad one a good one, but to make a good one better, or out of many good ones one principal good one."

The work was finished and published in 1611, with the following:

THE HOLY BIBLE,

Containing the Old Testament,

AND THE NEW:

Newly Translated out of the Original tongues: & with the former Translations diligently compared and revised, by his Majesty's special Commandment."

Approved to be read in Churches.

Imprinted at London by Robert Barker, Printer to the Kings most Excellent Majesty.

ANNO DOM. 1611.

This Bible Translation Timeline section of *For Love of the Book* is intended to familiarize the reader with Bible translation milestones and recognize the sacrifices made by many brave hearts. The purpose of *For Love of the Book* prevents the inclusion of the many English versions published after 1611.

Again I encourage you to read *Wide as the Waters: The Story of the English Bible and the Revolution It Inspired* by Benson Bobrick, a book that provides an excellent history of our English Bible.

V

WHAT OTHERS HAVE SAID

"In regard to this Great Book, I have but to say, it is the best gift God has given to man. All the good the Savior gave to the world was communicated through this book. But for it we could not know right from wrong. All things most desirable for man's welfare, here and hereafter, are to be found portrayed in it. To you I return my most sincere thanks for the very elegant copy of the great Book of God which you present."

— Abraham Lincoln, 16th US President
Oral reply upon presentation of a Bible by appreciative black citizens in Baltimore, September 7, 1864

"I consider an intimate knowledge of the Bible an indispensable quality of a well-educated man."

— Dr. Robert Millikan, physicist,
former President of the California Institute of Technology,
Nobel Peace Prize winner

"When you have read the Bible, you will know it is the Word of God, because you have found it the key to your own heart, your own happiness, and your own duty."

— Woodrow Wilson, 28th US President

"... By this time I clearly understood that Jesus Christ was the Creator of the universe, that He paid the price that only a sinless person could pay for all of my offenses against God, and that eternal life would be mine if I would receive His pardon and give Him His rightful place of authority over my life."

— *Dr. Hugh Ross, Astronomer, Ph.D.*
http://www.reasons.org/articles/hugh-ross-testimony

"The fundamental basis of this nation's laws was given to Moses on the Mount. The fundamental basis of our Bill of Rights comes from the teaching we get from Exodus and St. Matthew, from Isaiah and St. Paul. I don't think we emphasize that enough these days. If we don't have the proper fundamental moral background, we will finally end up with a totalitarian government which does not believe in rights for anybody except the State."

— *Harry Truman, 33rd US President*
https://bit.ly/2GhFpV0

"... what the Apostle Paul calls the renewed mind. Out of a mind renewed by Jesus came the obvious. How could a scientist achieve his goal of discovering the absolute truths that govern the natural world without the blessing of the Author of those truths? For me now the true thrill of science is the search to understand a small corner of God's grand design, and to lay the glory for such discoveries at the Grand Designer's feet . . .

for the scientific mind, the Bible is wonderful if you read it from start to finish. It fits together with an astonishing consistency, which was the opposite of my secular perception. My early impressions were that it was rife with contradictions."

— *Dr. Raymond Damadian,*
Inventor of the first MR Scanning Machine (MRI)

"There came a time in my life when I doubted the divinity of the Scriptures, and I resolved as a lawyer and a judge I would try the Book as I would try anything in the courtroom, taking evidence for and against. It was a long, serious and profound study: and using the same principles of evidence in this religious matter as I always do in secular matters, I have come to the decision that the Bible is a supernatural Book, that it has come from God, and that the only safety for the human race is to follow its teachings."

*— Salmon P. Chase,
former U.S. Senator, Governor of Ohio,
Secretary of the Treasury,
and Chief Justice of the Supreme Court*

"We cannot read the history of our rise and development as a nation, without reckoning with the place the Bible has occupied in shaping the advances of the Republic. Where we have been the truest and most consistent in obeying its precepts, we have attained the greatest measure of contentment and prosperity. . . "

*— Franklin Roosevelt, 32nd US President,
http://www.presidency.ucsb.edu/ws/?pid=14960*

"Without God there could be no American form of government, nor an American way of life. Recognition of the Supreme Being is the first — the most basic — expression of Americanism. Thus, the founding fathers of America saw it, and thus with God's help, it will continue to be."

*— Dwight Eisenhower, 34th US President,
Remarks Recorded for the "Back-to-God" Program of the
American Legion, 2/20/1955, https://bit.ly/2nP5EqD*

"Men do not reject the Bible because it contradicts itself but because it contradicts them."

— Reverend E. Paul Hovey
https://bit.ly/2DNPgwx

"I have known ninety-five of the world's greatest men in my time, and of these eighty-seven were followers of the Bible. It is stamped with a Specialty of Origin, and an immeasurable distance separates it from all competitors"

— W.E. Gladstone
former Prime Minister of the United Kingdom

"The great reservoir of the power that belongs to God is His own Word the Bible. If we wish to make it ours, we must go to that Book. Yet people abound in the Church who are praying for power and neglecting the Bible. Men are longing to have power for bearing fruit in their own lives and yet forget that Jesus has said: "The seed is the Word of God" (Luke 8:11).

— R.A. Torrey

". . . includes all the wicked dead, from the days of Cain down to the last apostate from millennial glory. There will not be one there who has not passed through the article of death — not one there whose name has been set down in life's fair book — not one there that shall not be judged according to his own very deeds — not one there who shall not pass from the dread realities of the great white throne into everlasting horrors and torments of the lake that burneth with fire and brimstone. How awful! How terrible! How dreadful!"

— C.H. Mackintosh
Commenting on Revelation 20:11-15

VI

How Can the Bible Be Understood?

When studying the Bible, an inquiring mind is helpful. As you read, try to determine the what, why, and how. Get into the habit of asking questions and looking for answers. God's Spirit controlled the writer, and that Spirit had a purpose. Do not go into Bible study thinking that you need to pry something meaningful out of everything you read. Doing so may lead to misinterpretation. Successful students demonstrate patience and humility, and will have tranquil hearts with a thirst for knowing God's mind on the topic. The fewer preconceived notions and biases you have, the more you may learn.

Some portions of Scripture may appear to have more than one meaning or purpose. To assume that the author had one primary lesson to teach is best, and one primary lesson is what you should expect to find. Sometimes, discovering this lesson requires diligence. Do not be discouraged. Learn to appreciate the exercise. The lightbulb moments are precious!

Many people do not read the Bible because they feel it is hard to comprehend. As with anything worth learning, your understanding will be proportional to the amount of time you spend reading and studying. Nonetheless, even seasoned Bible students will find tough subjects in Scripture. Here are a few suggestions to help you.

You Must Understand the Gospel

The Gospel Is:*

- Jesus died so that your sin could be forgiven.
- Jesus was buried and came back to life to prove His power over death.

Jesus' Death Paid the Penalty for Your Sin

Jesus surrendered His life voluntarily to pay the penalty for your sin. Christ's sinlessness made it possible for Him to take your guilt and condemnation upon Himself. The lamb in the Exodus Passover is a representation, or archetype, of what Jesus did 1500 years later. Death passed over the Hebrews when that lamb was slain, and its blood placed on the door posts. The second death will pass over those who turn from sin and trust Christ! (*Revelation 20:14 & 21:8*)

The Exodus Passover Archetype:

"Your lamb shall be without blemish, a male of the first year: ye shall take it out from the sheep, or from the goats: . . .

And they shall take of the blood, and strike it on the two side posts and on the upper door post of the houses, wherein they shall eat it. . .

and when I see the blood, I will pass over you,"
—Exodus 12:5-7, 13

The New Testament Fulfillment:

"But with the precious blood of Christ, as of a lamb without blemish and without spot:"
—1 Peter 1:19

"And almost all things are by the law purged with blood; and without shedding of blood is no remission . . .

he appeared to put away sin by the sacrifice of himself."
—Hebrews 9:22, 26

Jesus' Resurrection Proves He is God

Jesus was buried and came back to life on the third day. His resurrection proves He is God and has power over death. The resurrection validates Christ's ministry, deity, and absolute sovereignty over His creation.

To apply this sacrifice to your life, you must change your mind about and turn from sin, and believe what He did for you. In so doing, your sin will be paid for; you will not be held accountable for that sin. God will forget your sin, your debt will be paid — and the guilt? Gone.

Be Sure of Your Relationship with God

- Can you explain what sin is?
- Do you believe you are a sinner?
- Do you desire a life that is pleasing to God?
- Do you want to follow Christ?

- Do you believe Jesus Christ is God the Son who became a man and that He never sinned?

- Do you believe that to pay for your sins, He died and came back to life?

- If you answered yes to these questions, talk to God and in your words: Tell Him, "I realize what sin is, and I admit that I am a sinner."

If you do not believe you are a sinner, — ****STOP**** — Go to: **http://forloveofthebook.com/1** for help understanding your sin nature.

Before proceeding to the next point, you must believe that you are a sinner and desire to follow Christ. It may help to get a Bible and read Romans 3.

- Tell Him: "Jesus, I believe what You did for me."

- Ask Him: "Please forgive me."

I cannot stress enough the importance of the previous questions and responding positively. In this way, you receive God's pardon from the guilt and penalty of sin and the promise of eternal life.

If you turn from sin and to God, confess that you believe what Christ did for you, and ask Him to forgive you, you are now a Christian: You are born-again (the New Birth) — you are saved. Because of that prayer, you now have God's Holy Spirit living in you. You are assured of eternal life and a home in Heaven.

Not only will the Lord forgive you, He will completely forget your sin.

"I, even I, am he that blotteth out thy transgressions for mine own sake, and will not remember thy sins."

—Isaiah 43:25

"He will turn again, he will have compassion upon us; he will subdue our iniquities; and thou wilt cast all their sins into the depths of the sea."

—Micah 7:19

"As far as the east is from the west, so far hath he removed our transgressions from us."

—Psalms 103:12

Your salvation does not depend on you or your goodness. Your salvation depends on Christ, and He gave us special promises concerning this marvelous gift. No one can take this from you and you cannot lose it.

"Therefore by the deeds of the law there shall no flesh be justified in his sight: for by the law is the knowledge of sin."

—Romans 3:20

"Knowing that a man is not justified by the works of the law, but by the faith of Jesus Christ, even we have believed in Jesus Christ, that we might be justified by the faith of Christ, and not by the works of the law: for by the works of the law shall no flesh be justified."

—Galatians 2:16

"For by grace are ye saved through faith; and that not of yourselves: it is the gift of God:

Not of works, lest any man should boast."
—Ephesians 2:8-9

"And as Moses lifted up the serpent in the wilderness, even so must the Son of man be lifted up:

That whosoever believeth in him should not perish, but have eternal life.

For God so loved the world, that he gave his only begotten Son, that whosoever believeth in him should not perish, but have everlasting life.

For God sent not his Son into the world to condemn the world; but that the world through him might be saved.

He that believeth on him is not condemned: but he that believeth not is condemned already, because he hath not believed in the name of the only begotten Son of God."
—John 3:14-18

"And I give unto them eternal life; and they shall never perish, neither shall any man pluck them out of my hand."
—John 10:28

"These things have I written unto you that believe on the name of the Son of God; that ye may know that ye have eternal life, and that ye may believe on the name of the Son of God."
 —1 John 5:13

Scripture teaches that people who have not experienced the new birth cannot be expected to understand His Word. *A genuine desire to know God's Word must be preceded by the same desire to know Him and possess His forgiveness and restoration.*

"But the natural man receiveth not the things of the Spirit of God: for they are foolishness unto him: neither can he know them, because they are spiritually discerned."
 —1 Corinthians 2:14

Develop a Habit

Read the Bible daily. Throughout the day, ponder on what you read. Serious students of the Bible will find the Holy Spirit guiding their efforts. If a passage confuses you, take a break and think about it. Pray about it. You can always come back to it another time.

Scripture is Its Own Best Interpreter

The concept of using Scripture to interpret Scripture is mentioned in 2 Peter 1:19-21 and in 1 Corinthians 2:13. Locate other verses that discuss the same topic or situation. Passages can become clearer when you read what another author had to say about the subject. A Bible cross reference will help.

Use Commentaries Sparingly

Commentaries can be helpful, but they can also mislead you. I prefer *Believer's Bible Commentary* by William MacDonald combined with some caution.

Connect with a Bible-Believing Church

Find a place of worship where its leadership and members put God's Word first. Be sure they teach the Bible honestly and well. Look for humility and kindness in these people. Being involved in a local church is an essential part of a successful Christian life. For help finding a church, go to: **http://forloveofthebook.com/2**

Use Bible Software

e-Sword is a personal favorite. This computer application integrates with many free Bible study tools.

Use an Audio Bible

Consider purchasing Alexander Scourby's** reading of the King James Bible. Listening and reading at the same time will help you to stay focused. Mr. Scourby's voice is without equal. You will be surprised at how much reading you will accomplish with this method. Look for ISBN 978-1-59856-359-7.

*A comprehensive explanation of the gospel is available at: http://forloveofthebook.com/gospel.htm

**Scourby, Alexander. Holy Bible (King James Version) Audio CD.

"It is necessary for the welfare of the nation that men's lives be based on the principles of the Bible. No man, educated or uneducated, can afford to be ignorant of the Bible."

— Theodore Roosevelt

Conclusion

Never has a book been able to do what the Bible does. The Bible provides truth that results in permanently changed hearts, and when obeyed, the Bible preserves lives, souls, and nations. The Bible enables us to see our inherent nature and explains the only way that will free us from sin's bondage and take away sin's guilt and punishment.

We cannot doubt that the original manuscripts were of ages long past. They were out of sight and out of mind for hundreds, sometimes thousands of years, tucked away in various obscure places around the globe. Ordinary folk and researchers have found them in deserted caves near the Dead Sea, in synagogues, and in forgotten rooms of monasteries throughout Europe and North Africa. In some of these places, the documents had been hidden for centuries, covered with the dust of nearly two-thousand years.

Highly educated and ardent champions worked tirelessly to preserve the texts and bring them together to form the canon of Scripture, the Holy Bible. As you reflect on the sacrifices made throughout history to assure God's Word would be available to you, ask yourself, *Is the Bible important?* No document has ever existed that has had such power to influence men and women for good. Many passionate souls have labored against this Book, yet it has never ceased to draw people out of darkness and into its marvelous light.

The Bible is blessed with supernatural power by the source of all power, The Lord God, Creator of heaven and earth, the sea, and all that is in them.

No other book has such a pedigree. Its light will shine forever.

"The words of the LORD are pure words: as silver tried in a furnace of earth, purified seven times.

Thou shalt keep them, O LORD, thou shalt preserve them from this generation for ever."

—Psalm 12:6, 7

"Bad men cannot make good citizens. It is impossible that a nation of infidels or idolaters should be a nation of freemen. It is when a people forget God that tyrants forge their chains. A vitiated state of morals, a corrupted public conscience, is incompatible with freedom. No free government, or the blessings of liberty, can be preserved to any people but by a firm adherence to justice, moderation, temperance, frugality, and virtue; and by a frequent recurrence to fundamental principles."

— Patrick Henry

The Early North American Bibles

Before the American Revolution, the King of England issued licenses to publish English Bibles. To print them otherwise was illegal. The only licensed presses were at Oxford, Cambridge, and at a printer's in Scotland.

At the time of American independence, United States printers had produced only two editions of the Bible.

1661-63   The first American Bible was translated into the Algonquin Indian language by John Eliot and published by Marmaduke Johnson, Cambridge, Massachusetts. He released the New Testament in 1661 and the entire Bible in 1663. You can read more about Mr. Eliot's missionary work at GreatSite.com.

1743   The second American Bible and the first foreign-language Bible printed in America was that of Christopher Saur, printed in German in Germantown, Pennsylvania. Saur issued one thousand copies.

1782   Robert Aitken published the first English Bible in America. Congress commended his work and issued an endorsement for the Bible. This Bible is rare. Only fifty copies were known to exist in 1940.

1790   William Young released a small King James Bible that could fit in a coat pocket.

1791	Isaiah Thomas published the first illustrated Bible in Worcester, Massachusetts.
	Isaac Collins printed five thousand of the first Family Bibles. Less than a hundred exist today. He did not include the dedication to King James saying, ". . . and perhaps on some accounts improper to be continued in an American edition."
1792	Hodge & Campbell published Brown's Bible, a self-interpreting Bible containing Reverend John Brown's analysis and notes. President George Washington owned this Bible.
1796	Jacob R. Berriman published editions of the Bible containing American engravings done in the 1700s.
1798	John Thompson printed the first "hot-pressed" Bible that up to that time was the largest.
1789-1808	Charles Thomson and Jane Aitken
	Charles Thomson produced the first English translation of the Old Testament Greek Septuagint and the first modern English translation of the New Testament. He spent twenty years improving his works and looking for someone to print them. Jane Aitken, daughter of printer Robert Aitken, was chosen for the task and became the first woman to publish a Bible.

1818	The three epistles of the Apostle John were published in the Delaware Indian language. Christian Frederick Dencke, a Moravian missionary, completed this work.
1833	Noah Webster published a minor revision of the King James Version.

He replaced a few difficult words and made some minor grammatical changes. |
1837	First "raised letters" American copy of the New Testament for the blind; funded by the American and Massachusetts Bible Societies; completed at New England Asylum for the Blind
1841-42	The American Bible Society printed the complete Bible in raised letters.
1858	The American Bible Society published 300 distinctive Bibles whose covers were imprinted with: "Presented by Russell, Majors & Waddell – 1858". These men were operators of the Pony Express mail route. Each Pony Express rider was given his own Bible to carry with him. A small number of copies survive.
1859-61	The New Testament was printed in the Cree language, followed by the entire Bible.

Reverend William Mason and his Cree wife Sophia had translated the work. |
| 1860 | The New Testament was published in the Cherokee language. |

References

Religious Landscape Study-Pew Forum on Religious and Public Life.
http://www.pewforum.org/religious-landscape-study

Martin, Ernest L, Ph.D. *Restoring the Original Bible*, Chapter 6: "The Design of the Old Testament." Associates for Scriptural Knowledge
http://www.askelm.com/restoring/res006.htm

Authenticity of Old Testament Scripture.
http://www.kenscustom.com/bible/authen.html

Information Helping you Judge the Bible for Yourself.
http://www.provethebible.net/T2-Integ/B-0601.htm

Kenyon, Sir Frederic G. *Our Bible and the Ancient Manuscripts*, Chapter 4: "History of the Text and Its Translations."
https://archive.org/details/ourbibleandanci00kenygoog

Library of Congress. Scrolls from the Dead Sea: The Qumran Community.
https://www.loc.gov/exhibits/scrolls/late.html

Essenes.
https://en.wikipedia.org/wiki/Essenes

The Seed Company. *The History of Bible Translation*.
https://bit.ly/2pz8ReV

Connolly, K.W. *The Indestructible Book*. Grand Rapids: Baker Books, 1996.

Bobrick, Benson. *Wide as the Waters: The Story of the English Bible and the Revolution It Inspired.* New York: Penguin Group, 2002.

Septuagint.
https://en.wikipedia.org/wiki/Septuagint

Joseph, Jr., Ken. *Amazing Discovery in China Changes Christian History in Asia.*
http://www.atour.com/religion/docs/20011114a.html

Plumptre, Edward H. *English Translations of the Bible.*
http://www.bible-researcher.com/plumptre1.html

Dixon, Richard W. *History of the Church of England: From the Abolition of The Roman Jurisdiction.* Vol. II, p.76.
https://bit.ly/2G4Uk1y

Great Bible.
https://en.wikipedia.org/wiki/Great_Bible

The American Minute.
http://www.americanminute.com

The Bibles of Colonial America.
http://www.greatsite.com/timeline-english-bible-history/colonial-bibles.html

Chronological History of the Holy Bible.
http://clausenbooks.com/bible1900.htm

McClintock, John. *Cyclopaedia of Biblical, Theological, and Ecclesiastical Literature,* Vol. III, p. 208.
https://bit.ly/2l1rWo3

And

The Bible

About the Author

Rodger Copp became a Christian in 1974 when he realized that it was not baptism that restored a broken relationship with his Creator, but repentance and trusting Christ that united him with his God.

Following a four year commitment in the military, Rodger attended Bible school. Since then, he has taught and preached God's Word on many occasions and in many venues. Although he has never been a pastor, he desires to be one when he grows up.

Rodger has a natural ability to teach. However, by day he is a systems administrator, so his outreach has primarily been to those who are IT-challenged. Nevertheless, he gets the most enjoyment from teaching the Bible. During these opportunities he is the most engaged and animated.

Rodger lives with the wife of his youth, Cindy, in a cozy log home overlooking Lake Superior. He spends his free time working on things of eternal value, playing in the woods, or decreasing the size of the honey-do list. Rodger and Cindy have been blessed with two fine children and the same number of grandchildren.

ftlotbook@gmail.com

For additional copies visit:

http://forloveofthebook.com